**The local search series**

Editor: Mrs Molly Harrison MBE

# Rivers and Canals

*A formal portrait of James Brindley, the great eighteenth century canal builder, who built the Bridgewater Canal, opened in 1761.*

# Rivers and Canals

Rowland W. Purton

London, Henley and Boston   Routledge & Kegan Paul

'. . . all the business of life is to endeavour to find out what you don't know by what you do'

John Whiting *Marching Song*

*First published 1972*
*by Routledge & Kegan Paul Ltd*
*39 Store Street*
*London WC1E 7DD*
*Broadway House, Newtown Road*
*Henley-on-Thames, Oxon RG9 1EN* and
*9, Park Street, Boston*
*Mass. 02108, USA*
*Reprinted 1976*
*Filmset and printed in Great Britain by*
*BAS Printers Limited, Wallop, Hampshire*

*ISBN 0 7100 7439 5 (c)*
*ISBN 0 7100 7440 9 (l)*

# The local search series

Editor: Mrs Molly Harrison MBE

Many boys and girls enjoy doing research about special topics and adding drawings, photographs, tape-recordings and other kinds of evidence to the notes they make. We all learn best when we are doing things ourselves.
The books in this series are planned to help in this kind of 'project' work. They give basic information but also encourage the reader to find out other things; they answer some questions but ask many more; they suggest interesting things to do, interesting places to visit, and other books that can help readers to enjoy their finding out and to look more clearly at the world around them.

M.H.

# Acknowledgments

The author and publishers would like to thank those listed below for permission to reproduce illustrations: Aerofilms Ltd, Barnaby's Picture Library, The Bowater Organization, British Waterways Board, Central Electricity Generating Board, The Commissioner of Police for the Metropolis, National Film Board of Canada, The Trustees of the National Gallery, London, Popperfoto, Port of London Authority, Port of Manchester, Radio Times Hulton Picture Library, Stichting 'Havenbelangen', Rotterdam.
Photographs not otherwise acknowledged were taken by the author.

# Contents

# Editor's preface

Nobody in the British Isles lives far from either a river or a canal. Whether you are in a city, or a small town, or in the country there is moving water not far away. Rivers and canals are varied and always changing. Every month, every season, each year is different, so there is always something new to see if you know what to look for.

This book is written to help you to enjoy using your eyes and ears when you visit one of our 'inland waterways' and to think about what you find. It shows you many things you may never have noticed before and – it can help you to find out for yourself.

If you are planning to do a project on a river or a canal you will have to use your eyes and your imagination. You will need to talk to local people and keep an eye on the local paper, to find out how things have changed and whether there are any plans for the future. And when you are on holiday you will find it interesting to visit other waterways and compare them with your own.

Most canals are quiet places now, but this was not always so. When they were first built people argued and complained about them, just as they do about our motorways now; but before long they were busy, important trade routes and people began to wonder how they managed without them – just as they do about the motorways.

Perhaps you have thought of rivers and canals as being just 'nature' or 'geography' or 'sport', but when you have read this book you may begin to see that there is history there too, and fine architecture, and art, literature and music. There are interests and pleasures to be found from every river and canal if we look carefully.

M.H.

# Your project

1

*Where to begin your project*

*Exploring rivers and canals*

*Assembling your material*

If you are intending to make a study of rivers and canals, you may wonder where to begin. Perhaps you think of great rivers such as the Thames, the Rhine or the Amazon, or of canals such as the Grand Union or the Panama. These may well come into your study later but you should forget them for the present.

Your project should not rely upon book knowledge but upon first hand experience. So go along to your nearest waterway and take a closer look at it. You may have seen it on many occasions and think this unnecessary. But have you ever really looked at it? Have you ever asked yourself where it comes from and where it goes to? Have you ever wondered why that bridge is in that particular position or what those locks are for? Have you noted the craft that use it, the plants that grow by it or the industries that depend upon it? In fact that very piece of water may be the sole reason why your town is there at all and, if it were able to speak, would probably have many an interesting tale to tell.

You may like to write your project entirely about your local river or canal, tracing its course from end to end through lush green countryside and industrial towns. You could note its place in history and particularly in the history of your town. You could see how many interesting things you could discover – and you could no doubt find many within walking or cycling distance of your starting point.

On the other hand, you may like to compare your local waterway with those in other parts of Britain or of the world. If so, do not forget the value of your own exploration. Clearly you will have to use books and a glance through a few before you

*Manchester Ship Canal runs beside the River Mersey at Runcorn, Cheshire.*

start will give you some ideas as to what to look for and what you may find of particular interest. This is the aim of this book. It is not a book about rivers and canals: it is a book to help *you* to find out for *yourself* about rivers and canals. It gives a little information but suggests many lines of discovery which you may follow. Obviously you will not be able to follow them all. Use the ones which are of the most interest to you and forget the rest.

This is a large subject and you will be wise if you make a plan of your work before you begin, noting those points about which you hope to write and for which you think you can find suitable pictures. Look at the contents page of this book and see one way that this may be done. When you have made a plan try to keep to it even though you find other interesting facts. You do not want to end up with a jumble of odd pieces of information. Of course your project will consist of other things than a book – models, drawings, paintings, specimens, photographs and so on.

Is your main interest in rivers or in canals? Rivers are natural waterways, though many have been improved by man: canals are man-made to assist trade and communications. Sometimes a canal runs beside a river but gives water deep enough for the craft that use it and has no mud flats, horseshoe bends, rapids

*Tottenham locks on the navigable Lea waterway.*

or other natural hazards as a river has. Canals took a lot of hard work to build and therefore were made no wider or deeper than was necessary: rivers flow through many kinds of country and change from small streams to broad rivers. Rivers find their own route as they make their way seaward: canals follow the route which was planned for them, often passing through tunnels or up flights of steps called locks. We shall return to all of these later. Your choice may depend upon whether your nearest waterway is a river or a canal and the kind of things you can see for yourself. Again, whichever you are studying will be affected by where you live. A town waterway may be very different from a country one. For example the River Lea leaves the countryside behind as it flows through an industrial area of London. The locks keep back the water so that it becomes a 'navigable waterway' with barges carrying goods to and from the Thames. The banks of the river were built up for use as a tow path from which horses could tow the barges and also to provide firm landings for the cargoes. One notices the riverside industries – the concrete workings, the gas works and pylons carrying electricity from the power station. Within a mile or so are timber wharves, factories, reservoirs and water works. It is very much an industrial scene, yet within a few miles the same river flows

*Girder railway bridge and concrete road bridge spanning the Great Ouse.*

through attractive countryside.

If you live in a country village or town, your nearest river may be more like the Great Ouse which flows through open fenland country. Sedges and waterlilies grow near the banks which are a mass of plant life providing homes for many wild creatures. It is a waterway with little industry but which is much used for boating holidays and fishing.

These are but two examples. Your local river or canal may be quite different from either – but it may be a starting point from which you can move on to make an interesting study of rivers or canals or both. You might find it worth visiting more than one river or canal to see how they differ and what they have in common before you begin working on your project.

You will not be able to see everything for yourself and you will find many books on rivers and canals from which you can obtain information. Do not allow yourself to become tied to one book. Use a selection and compare the information given. Above all, remember that if you only produce information from books you will have a poor and dull study. Your project needs to show what *you* have seen or collected or discovered and what conclusions *you* have drawn.

Once you have drawn up a rough outline of your project, keep your eyes open for anything that may be useful. You will need plenty of pictures if it is to be attractive. Picture postcards can be used and colourful scenes appear in holiday brochures and in magazines.

But do not depend only on what you can find. If you have a camera, take it with you on your expeditions and photograph anything that may be suitable. Make sketches, drawings and paintings of objects of interest. You may feel that you are not much of a photographer or artist and that pictures you find are much better than your own. You may be right but you can take some pride in your efforts and, in any case, your photographs and sketches show that you have made first-hand observations instead of finding all your information from other people's work.

Look also for poems, copies of paintings of rivers or canals, sayings or quotations, newspaper cuttings and anything else which may add interest to your project. Again, do not forget your notebook and pencil. Note anything worth remembering. Take it with you whenever you explore your river or canal. It is better to take notes than to rely upon your memory.

Take care when exploring the river or canal bank because there are many dangers there. Watch your footing because the bank may be muddy and slippery. Make sure that you step on firm ground: it is not always easy to tell where a river bank ends and the water begins. The water itself can also be dangerous so always treat all water with extreme caution. Remember, too, that the river bank may be private property and you should get permission before walking there. If in doubt always ask.

Finally, remember that many a good piece of work has been spoilt by bad layout and not enough attention to detail. Try to make your work look as attractive as possible. Do not overcrowd the pages but allow margins and also space between pictures and writing. Make sure that all your illustrations have titles so that the reader is in no doubt as to what they are. Mount any pictures carefully and take care with your modelling. Find out whether there are any special rules about presenting your study and keep to them. If you are able to choose for yourself, you will probably find it best to use loose pages. You can always rearrange or rewrite these if necessary without spoiling the general appearance. If your study is worth doing, these small points are important.

# 2 Looking at rivers

*How a river grows up*

*The appearance and course of a river*

*River names*

If you take a close look at your river, you will probably notice two important things about it. Firstly, it is constantly moving toward the sea and secondly, it twists and turns with very few straight stretches or *reaches*. The river has probably followed a very similar course for thousands of years. It was no doubt the route which it found the easiest, though not the shortest, from the mountains or hills to the sea.

During its journey, a river continually grows and changes. At first it is probably a lively stream, splashing over boulders and cascading down the mountains to join with similar streams and

*Peaceful River Ouse flows through Bedfordshire.*

so form a small river in the valley below.
Several of these small rivers may join to form a larger river which winds its way more slowly across the flatter country on its way to the sea. At this stage the river is likely to be deep enough to cover any boulders and to appear as a slow-moving mass of water as, for example, the Great Ouse does as it passes through Bedfordshire with some seventy odd miles to travel to the sea.
Near the sea a river is at its broadest. Industries of many kinds may be found on its banks; ships bring their cargoes from far-away places; and the river becomes a centre of commerce. Here the river may even appear to flow in the wrong direction as the rising tide forces water up the estuary. Then, as the tide turns, the water races out even faster to leave mud flats on either side of the river.
You might like to make a study of your own river to follow its

*Ships moored in Woolwich Reach, River Thames.*

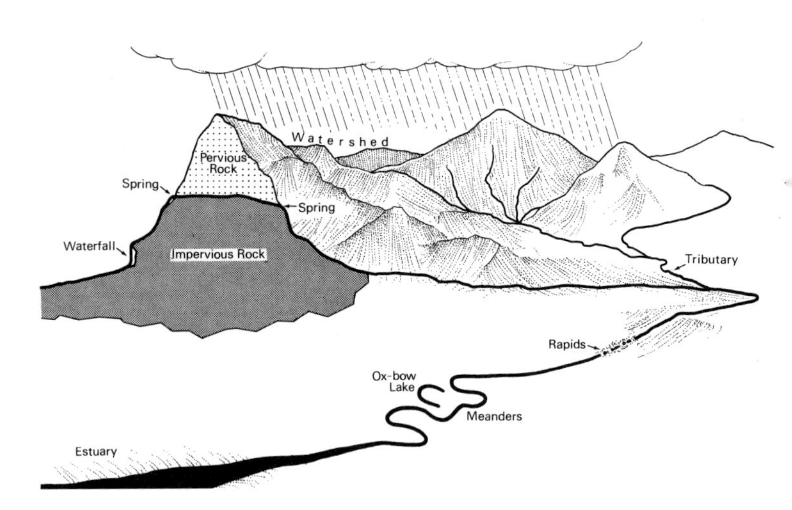


*Parts of a river.*

course and discover how it grows and changes. You will find some useful information from one-inch Ordnance Survey maps. Where is the source of the river? How high above sea level is the ground at the source? Is it in mountainous or hilly country? What other small rivers join it?

You could then see where the land levels out and check whether the contour lines on the map give any clues as to why the river follows that particular course. Discover also whether it has an estuary with a commercial port. Once you have plotted the course, see how many photographs you can find of the river at various stages. How does it change? Why?

A study of the river will lead to the discovery of many other things. Perhaps you have noticed the part played by the river in the 'water cycle' of nature. Sea and lake water is evaporated by the sun. The clouds which are formed rise to pass over the mountains. As they do so, the vapour is cooled and falls as rain on the mountains. This rain forms the rivers which carry the water back to the sea so that the whole process can begin again. A diagram to show this process would be interesting in your project.

As the rain falls on the mountains it may soak into the rock or it may run off. Water can soak into *pervious* rocks but not into *impervious* rocks. See how many examples of each you can name. When water soaks through and then reaches impervious rock it must come out of the mountain side. This is a *spring*. Springs and streams will be on one side of a mountain range

or the other. This mountain range which divides the water so that rivers flow in opposite directions is a *watershed*.
Water always finds its own path from the highest to the lowest level. It carries with it small particles of soil or rock so that in time a channel is worn away. Sometimes the water meets hard rock and tumbles over the edge to form a *waterfall*. You could find other names given to waterfalls such as *force* or *cataract* and discover where such names occur. You could also find out about some of the famous waterfalls of the world such as Victoria Falls (Rhodesia) and Niagara Falls (Canada and USA). Many rivers also have *rapids*. These are not waterfalls. What are they and how are they caused? Once the river reaches more level ground it may *meander* or follow a winding course. Try to discover where the word 'meander' comes from.

*River Clyde in the Lowther Hills. Note the meanders in the flat valley bottom and the deposits on the inside of the river bends.*

As a river flows it slowly washes away the bank on the outside of a bend and leaves a deposit of silt or rock on the inside. In time the river may break through the bank and take a short cut, leaving the former course as a lake called an *oxbow* lake. At last the river reaches the sea. If it is a small river this is known as the 'mouth': if it is a larger one it is called an 'estuary'. If the land around the estuary is flat the estuary may be very wide. At high tide, when the sea is flowing into the estuary, the whole may be filled with water. As the tide goes out (ebbs), the channel along which the river flows can be seen between the mud flats. This channel must be clearly marked if the estuary is used by ships. See if you can find out how channels are marked. (See also page 68.) Beneath the water in an estuary there are also many sand banks which have been built up gradually by the silt carried down by the river. This is because the silt which can be carried along in fast-flowing water drops when the water is slowed down by meeting the sea.

In some parts of the world there are rivers whose estuaries have become so built up that the water must force its way through. Instead of one outlet to the sea they have several channels. A river mouth built up like this becomes a *delta*. You might like to find out how a delta became so named and also make a study of one or more of the famous deltas of the world:

| | |
|---|---|
| The Nile in Egypt | The Niger in . . . . |
| The . . . . in India | The Indus in . . . . |
| The Orinoco in . . . . | The . . . . in Burma |

We have seen that on the whole a river makes its own course and sometimes changes it. Occasionally man alters a river for his own convenience. At Bristol, for example, the Avon was diverted along the New Cut so that the old river could become an enclosed dock. In Australia an ambitious scheme in the Snowy Mountains caused a river to be diverted through tunnels so that it flowed down the opposite side of the mountains and thus irrigated dry land.

These are fairly modern examples but we know from early records that King Alfred had the course of the River Lea altered and thus trapped some Danish ships. Perhaps you can find other examples of ways in which man has changed the nature of a river.

The names of rivers are interesting. There are several rivers named *Avon*, the Celtic word for 'river'. Many names, Axe, Exe, Esk, Usk come from the Celtic *Isca* meaning 'water'. Place names also come from their positions on rivers. No explanation is needed for places ending in *-ford* or *-bridge*. *Pont-* is Welsh for 'bridge'. Places standing near a river mouth may be named *-mouth*, e.g. Plymouth – 'Mouth of the Plym'. The Scottish equivalent is *Inver-* and the Welsh *Aber-*, e.g. Inverness, Aberystwyth. Aberystwyth means 'the mouth of the winding stream'. It would be interesting to add a list of such meanings to your project.

You might also like to note how rivers are affected by the seasons – swollen with the spring thaw, flooding after heavy rain or very low in drought. Do British rivers freeze in winter? Is a river more or less likely to freeze than a pond? How are frozen rivers put to good use in Canada? And what about permanently frozen rivers or *glaciers*, which creep slowly down the mountains? How can a river be otherwise affected by its surroundings? Does the name 'Red River' suggest anything?

Take another look at your local river and see how many of these things you can apply to it.

# 3 Rivers and civilization

*Growth of towns at river crossings*

*Ancient civilizations, the Bible lands and religion*

*History, discovery, folk-lore and music*

Man discovered rivers long before there were towns and cities. No doubt he sometimes found these rivers a nuisance because they prevented him from travelling wherever he wanted to. To cross the river, he had either to swim or to wade across and so he tried to find a place where the river was shallow. Such a place was called a ford. Around these fords villages began to grow, some of which have since developed into towns. If a name of a town ends in *-ford* it tells us why it grew on that site. Some of these fords were named after people while others show what the fords were used for, like this:

Bedford – Beda's ford  Oxford – a ford for oxen
Stratford – a river crossing for a Roman road

Perhaps you could find out how others obtained their names. As time passed, bridges were built beside the fords. Some of the earliest were packhorse bridges wide enough only for a packhorse laden with goods. Others were wide enough to take carts or wagons pulled by horses. There was little traffic then and carts would not need to pass each other on the bridge, so bridges did not need to be wide. This is a great problem in these days and many an old bridge creates a bottle-neck for rush-hour or summer seasonal traffic. The bridge at St Ives, Huntingdonshire, is such a bridge. You will notice that the piers which support the arches point outward from the bridge to cut the water which flows beneath. These continue to the top of the bridge where they form triangular-shaped refuges for pedestrians to keep out of the way of traffic. This bridge like a number of others built in medieval times, has a chantry

*Bridge, completed in 1425 and partially rebuilt in 1716, with chapel and town quay at St Ives, Huntingdonshire.*

or chapel built in the centre. You might like to find out why it is there.

There are many kinds of bridge that cross rivers. Some appear in the pictures in this book (pages 2, 4, and 63). Other kinds cross canals (see page 25). Go out with your camera or your sketch pad and photograph or draw them: you will find many interesting ones. Perhaps you could classify them under these headings:

arch beam girder suspension cantilever
fortified bascule swing tubular transporter

Look to the right of the bridge on this page and you will see the town quay, now used by pleasure craft but once the place to which small ships could bring their cargoes. In the past the first bridge across the river from seaward marked the limit to which ships could sail. This point is known as the 'head of navigation'. Of course river craft can go further and the head of navigation for these is much higher up the river than for sea-going ships.

It is easy to see why towns grew around the bridges. Apart from being the meeting points of several roads they were the places at which ships had to be loaded and discharged and were therefore centres of commerce. If you have an old river-

Cutting rushes.

crossing in your town, you may still be able to find traces of old businesses which existed around the bridge or the town quay, possibly old warehouses, customs houses or boatyards. Look also for an old inn near the bridge which was used by travellers. In other parts the river crossing had to be made by means of a ferry. Many rivers have inns named 'The Ferry Boat', which tell us that here people had to cross the river by boat. Some of these ferries still remain, though they are not of such importance as they were in days before the motor car. There are still various forms of ferry today and this again could be interesting to study. Here are some suggestions:

Ferry boats and boatmen
Chain ferries
Passenger ferries (e.g. Liverpool – Birkenhead)
Vehicle ferries (e.g. Woolwich, London)

Many people have found rivers useful for trade and commerce others have found that the river could provide a different kind of living: for example, rushes are still cut from the side of the river as they have been for hundreds of years. What are they used for? Are there any country crafts in your area which are dependent upon the river? We shall look at riverside industries in chapter 6.

*An irrigation wheel in Syria.*

Rivers have also provided water for the land and are used by local farmers for watering fields. In dry lands water from rivers is used for *irrigation*. In some places irrigation ditches are cut into which the water may flow. It is still possible to see primitive water-wheels in the Middle East, or peasant farmers lifting water by means of a *shadoof* – a kind of bucket on a weighted pole. You could, if it interests you, make a study of irrigation methods, perhaps comparing the ancient methods with modern schemes such as those in South Australia or California.

You can see why all the great civilizations of the ancient world grew up in the river valleys – the flood water gave the most fertile land for the growing of crops. Several civilizations developed in the land between the rivers Tigris and Euphrates. There were the civilizations of Sumer and Babylonia with their cities at Ur and Babylon. In Babylon were the famous Hanging Gardens, one of the Seven Wonders of the Ancient World, to which water for the plants and lawns was pumped from the river Euphrates which passed through the city. Assyria with its capital Nineveh was further up the Tigris.

The civilization of Egypt developed along the banks of the Nile. The annual flooding of the Nile, caused by melting snows in Ethiopia, gave a rich layer of silt. Nowadays this flood water is controlled by the Aswan Dam.

Remember, too, that all of these rivers were highroads for trade. Basket boats or 'guffas' carried goods on the Tigris and wooden boats on the Nile.

In India the rivers Indus and Ganges were centres of civilization. Ancient cities, Mohenjo-daro and Harappa, dating from over 4,500 years ago, have been excavated on the Indus. In China people settled along the Hwang-Ho or Yellow River, so named from the yellow silt which it carried. It is also known as 'China's Sorrow' because so many thousands have drowned in its floods.

For Jewish and Christian people an important river in the Middle East is the Jordan, which flows through the Holy Land. It is not a large river like the others mentioned above but it did mark the boundary of the Promised Land and was crossed by Joshua and the Israelites (Joshua chapter 3, vv. 14–17). It features in the story of Elijah and Elisha (2 Kings chapter 2, vv. 7–8, 13–14) and it was in the Jordan that Naaman had to dip to be cured of leprosy (2 Kings chapter 5, vv. 1–15). But perhaps the great significance to Christians is that it was the river in which John the Baptist baptized people including Jesus Christ himself (St Mark chapter 1, vv. 1–11). If you wish to look further into the Biblical aspect of rivers you will find a concordance useful to look up references to the Jordan. Few other rivers are mentioned and then mainly because they formed boundaries. Here are some:

Euphrates Abana Pharpar Jabbok Kishon

Another river with special religious significance is the Ganges, the sacred river of the Hindus. Millions of Hindus gather at Varanasi (Benares) to bathe from the riverside steps known as the ghats.

Perhaps you would like to study the place of rivers in later history. Some of them provided natural frontiers between neighbouring countries. The Rhine, for example, has played a very important role in the history of Germany, France and other countries. It provided the best defence for the Romans against the barbarian tribes; it ran through the centre of Charlemagne's empire; and it has seen squabbles in more recent times between France and Germany who have each claimed its territory.

But along the Rhine are many castles, built high above the

river by those who wanted to control it – powerful nobles who could demand dues from all who passed that way. Castles like these are found on British rivers too. The nobles also found that the river formed a good defence, for a wide river could be better than a moat.

You could build a short history around such rivers as the Rhine, the Seine, the Danube or the Thames.

Again, rivers have played a vital role in the discovery of the world and in the opening up of new lands, especially those where overland travel was made almost impossible by dense jungle. You could perhaps find out about the use made by these explorers of the rivers mentioned.

Livingstone (Zambezi and Limpopo)
Mungo Park (Niger) Stanley (Congo)
Cartier (St Lawrence) Bruce (Nile)
La Salle (Mississippi)

In America in days when transport was difficult the rivers

*Famous race, in 1870, of the Mississippi steamers* Robt. E. Lee *and* Natchez, *from New Orleans to St Louis, a distance of 1210 miles.*

became the highways. Small towns grew up along the banks, aided considerably by a new invention – the steamboat. Wide American rivers like the Hudson and Mississippi had proved ideal testing grounds for ships with engines driven by steam. On the Mississippi they took the form of steamboats with two tall funnels and huge paddle wheels.

There was great rivalry between the steamboat owners which, in the 1830s, reached the stage of madness. Rival steamboats would race down the river. Some blew up when the steam pressure was raised too high; some were involved in collisions; and some even rammed their rivals with loss of life. The fuel used was wood and it was quite common to see flames belching from the funnels.

These steamboats became an important part of the American scene and the subject of story and song. Perhaps you recall Ben in *Tom Sawyer*, who imagined himself as the *Big Missouri* and its crew rolled into one:

> 'Stop her, sir! Ling-a-ling-ling.' The headway ran almost out, and he drew slowly towards the sidewalk. 'Ship up to back! Ling-a-ling-ling!' His arms straightened and stiffened down his sides. 'Set her back on the stabbard! Ling-a-ling-ling! Chow! ch-chow-wow-chow!' his right hand meantime describing stately circles, for it was representing a forty-foot wheel. 'Let her go back on the labbard! Ling-a-ling-ling! Chow-ch-chow-chow!' The left hand began to describe circles . . .

The author had been apprenticed to a river pilot and took his name, Mark Twain, from the call of the leadsman on the big-wheelers.

The Mississippi steamboat became more than a contribution to the growth of the townships; it also found its way into the folk music of the United States. Perhaps you know the song about Steamboat Bill or others about the Mississippi.

You might like to see how many songs you can discover with rivers as their subject. Here are some you could begin with:

'Old Father Thames' 'Song of the Clyde' 'Afton Water'
'Ol' Man River' 'River, stay 'way from my door'
'Song of the Volga Boatmen' 'Eton Boating Song'

You might possibly come across a copy of the 'Ballad of the Erie Canal'. There are several versions of it which were sung by the canal men as their horses plodded along the tow-path. Why do you think the men sang?

If you are collecting river songs, you might also like to collect poems about rivers. There are some that speak of particular rivers and others on more general themes. Then, of course, rivers have played a part in the folk-lore of countries through which they flow. Legends concerning the Rhine are also the subject of Wagner's operas. You could try to find out more about river legends and folk-lore including, perhaps, some of the imaginary rivers of Greek mythology.

Thus it can be seen that many rivers have been responsible for the growth of civilizations and have added gaiety and colour to the culture of the peoples living nearby and also to those from much further afield who have enjoyed the songs and the stories.

# 4 Canals of Britain and the world

*The canal age in Britain*

*Waterways and ship canals today*

*Canals and rivers in art*

From early times people knew how useful rivers could be as means of communication but they also discovered that rivers alone were not enough. At some times they were in flood and at others they were almost empty. In places there were rapids which could not be passed, and rivers did not always run where they were needed. The answer was to build small canals to by-pass dangers and longer ones to connect with other towns.

One of the earliest canals was completed in the third century B.C. to link the Nile with the Red Sea. Other early canal builders were the Chinese and the Romans. Britain's oldest canal is probably the Fossdyke, built by the Romans in the second century A.D. to provide a waterway between Lincoln and the Trent.

You could make an interesting study of these early canals, some of which were remarkable feats of engineering. The Grand Canal of China was over six hundred miles long and was a busy waterway. In Britain only two further canals were built before the middle of the eighteenth century. One, alongside the River Exe in Devon, was opened in 1566: the other, from Newry to Lough Neagh, Ireland, was opened in 1742.

The great age of canal building in Britain began when the Duke of Bridgewater wanted to move coal cheaply from his land at Worsley to customers in Manchester. To build a canal, he employed a millwright named James Brindley. In only two years the ten-mile Bridgewater Canal was built. It included a number of interesting features such as the famous Barton Aqueduct which carried the canal thirty-eight feet above the

*Telford's Pontcysyllte Aqueduct is 1007 ft long and carries the Ellesmere Canal 121 ft over the River Dee in Denbighshire.*

River Irwell. This canal, which was opened in 1761, proved an instant success so that people in many parts of Britain clamoured for canals to transport their manufactured goods and to provide links between the great towns and rivers.

These canals had all to be cut by hand. The labourers for these 'canal navigations' became known as 'navigators', a name which was shortened to 'navvies' and was later applied to other heavy manual labourers.

In the years which followed there were several famous canal engineers. Perhaps you could find out more about them, especially any whose work is found in your area.

James Brindley (see frontispiece)    Thomas Telford

John Rennie    William Jessop    Josiah Clowes

These canal engineers were faced with various problems. New canal cuts had to be made waterproof or the water would soak away. If the canal was cut through clay there was no problem but otherwise a lining of 'puddled' loam was needed. You could discover how this was done and whether this method is still used today. A water supply was also needed.

When the canal crossed a river or valley an *aqueduct* was built. A fine example is Telford's Pontcysyllte Aqueduct carrying the

Ellesmere Canal over the River Dee. Canal builders had to work out the route with care. Canals must be on one level or the water would run out. Brindley believed in following the contours, so his canals wind a little. Telford preferred straight canals with 'locks' to raise the water level.

## Locks and lifts

Locks are used on rivers too. For many years weirs have been built on rivers to hold back the water for working water mills (see pages 40–3). Beside the weir was a *flash lock* which could be opened to allow barges to pass. As the gate was opened, the barge would be swept through 'in a flash'. Barges proceeding up-river might be winched through. Another method frequently used in East Anglia was the *staunch* – a vertically rising gate. Both were known by the Chinese long ago and it was a Chinese canal builder, Ch'iao Wei-Yo who built two staunches close together in A.D. 983, thus forming the first lock. Perhaps you could discover more about flash locks, staunches, water-gates and half-locks.

The lock, or *pound lock*, is a chamber with gates at either end, and large enough for the craft that will use it. The gates are usually mitred gates, which are kept closed by the pressure of

*Lock and gates. Notice watermark in the lock and winding gear for the paddles in the lock gates.*

water above them. In the wooden gate is a sluice or *slacker* or *paddle*, which can be opened to allow water to fill the lock. When full the top gates can be opened by leaning against the balancing beams.

## How locks work

If you watch boats going through a lock, you will soon see how the lock works. If you help work it you will understand even better. The lock pictured on this page has one guillotine-type gate, used on rivers where flood water would push open mitre gates. This has no paddles but is raised slightly to allow water to pass beneath. Notice how the lock works: (a) the guillotine is raised to allow a boat to enter. This is warped (walked) through the lock to allow room for a second boat; (b) The guillotine is lowered to hold back the water (which

*How locks work.*

by-passes the lock); (c) After the paddles in the lower gates have been opened, the water level drops to that of the water below the lock; (d) The lower gates are opened to allow the boats out.

Sometimes a canal must climb a hill where one lock is not enough. In this case there may be a 'staircase' or 'flight' of locks. It is not uncommon to find a flight of five or more locks on a canal, perhaps leading one from the other. You might find a picture of the famous staircase of twenty-nine locks near Devizes with side ponds to provide a water supply. This staircase is at present disused. A lot of water is lost each time a lock is opened and on a canal this is serious. Perhaps you could find out more about locks and lock flights, also about the reservoirs necessary for replacing the canal water.

Other methods of lifting canal boats have also been tried. One was to move them overland on a slope or *inclined plane*. In some the water was let out of the lock so that the boat came to rest on a cradle which was hauled on wheels to a higher lock. In others the boat was raised or lowered in a tank or *caisson* of water. There were only small inclines in Britain but much larger ones overseas. The last British one ceased to be used in 1922. There are also lifts. One working in Britain is at Anderton in Cheshire. Boats in caissons are lifted fifty feet from the River Weaver to the Trent and Mersey Canal. You could make a very interesting study of locks, caissons, inclines and lifts, showing the advantages and disadvantages of each and explaining how counterbalanced lifts worked. Are they still used?

There is much of interest to be seen along canals. Notice firstly the tow-path along which horses walked to tow the boats. The horses had to have stables when they were not working, so look for the stable buildings by a tow-path. Are horses still used today? Are mechanical aids for towing used anywhere in Britain? Or overseas? Discover why the tow-path sometimes switches from one bank to the other.

## Bridges and ironwork

Look for the very lovely bridges, some of them of a kind only found on canals. Some were especially built to save unhitching the horse when the tow-path changed from one bank to the

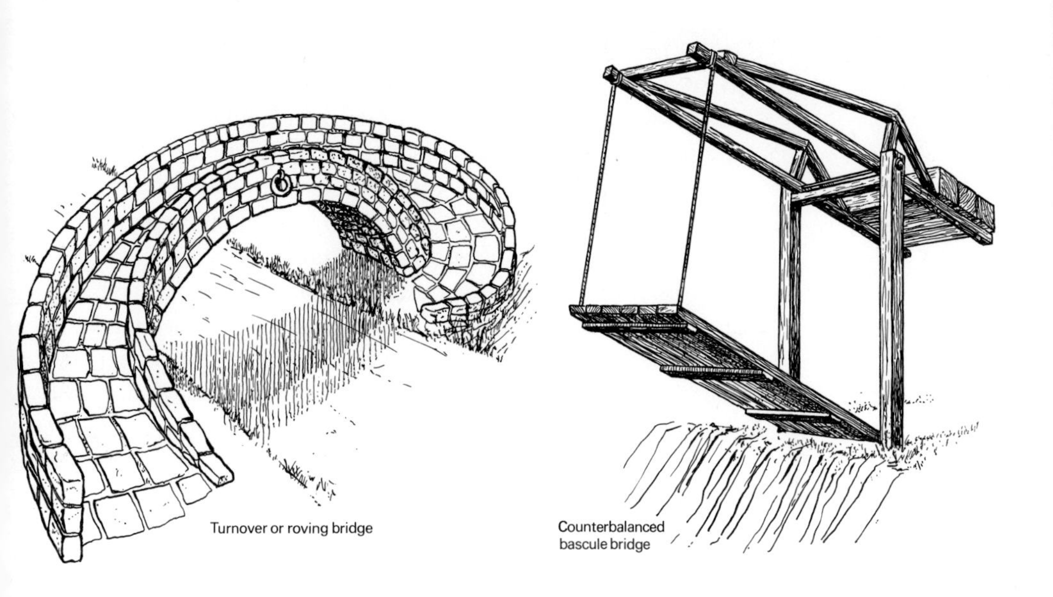


*Canal bridges.*

other. There were 'turnover' or 'roving' bridges where the horse passed over and then under the bridge and there were split bridges through which the rope could pass. There are hump-back bridges which now present a problem to motorists, bascule bridges which can be raised or lowered like a drawbridge and swing bridges which pivot on one bank.

You would find it worth while to draw or photograph some of these. What condition are they in? Some old bridges have been cemented over because it is cheaper than pointing them. What do you think about this? Discuss it with your friends.

Look on the bridges for interesting detail, such as attractive number plates and signs of wear where they have been cut by many tow-ropes. You will also find bridges made of iron and others with iron decorations. Canals were built at a time when decorative ironwork was fashionable. You can also find bollards, mile-stones, aqueducts and window frames all made of cast iron. Look on them to see where and by whom they were made.

The mile-stones were used in working out the tolls to be paid for the use of the canal. These were charged according to the weight of the cargo and the distance it was carried. You might find out more about tolls and how they were worked out. They were collected for the canal company at toll houses.

## Canal buildings

These toll houses are some of the interesting buildings to be seen beside canals. Many are octagonal in shape with windows facing along the cut in both directions. Look too for attractive cottages for lock-keepers and for pump houses which housed the machinery that kept the water at the correct level.

Other buildings which played a vital role in the lives of the canal people were the inns, the names of many of which are interesting. The inn-keeper was more than a publican: he was the man who passed information or got help. Look at any of these inns and compare the services provided then and now – stables for horses, taps for fresh water, rubbish tips and moorings.

## Tunnels

You will sometimes find that a canal disappears into a tunnel. Canal builders sometimes found it easier to build a tunnel through a hill than a flight of locks over it. Some were quite long. The longest at present in use is the Blisworth tunnel on the Grand Union Canal, which is 3,075 yds long. In order to save building costs, tunnels were built wide enough for the boats, but without a tow-path. Horses were led over the hill whilst the men 'walked' the boat through the tunnel by lying on special boards and walking against the walls. This was known as 'legging'. Some men earned their living as 'leggers' to be hired at the tunnels.

In time, steam tugs took over from the 'leggers'. You could discover the advantages and disadvantages of these. Think about cost, speed, safety, noise, pollution.

## Britain's waterways

Many of the waterways are still in use today and provide a useful means of communication. Some of the others are not used at present but may be re-opened for pleasure purposes. Of the principal waterways of England, some are rivers which have been made suitable for barge traffic. They are known as 'navigations'. Some are broad canals on which large barges can travel: others are narrow canals suitable only for the narrow

(*opposite*)
*Connected waterways of Britain today.*

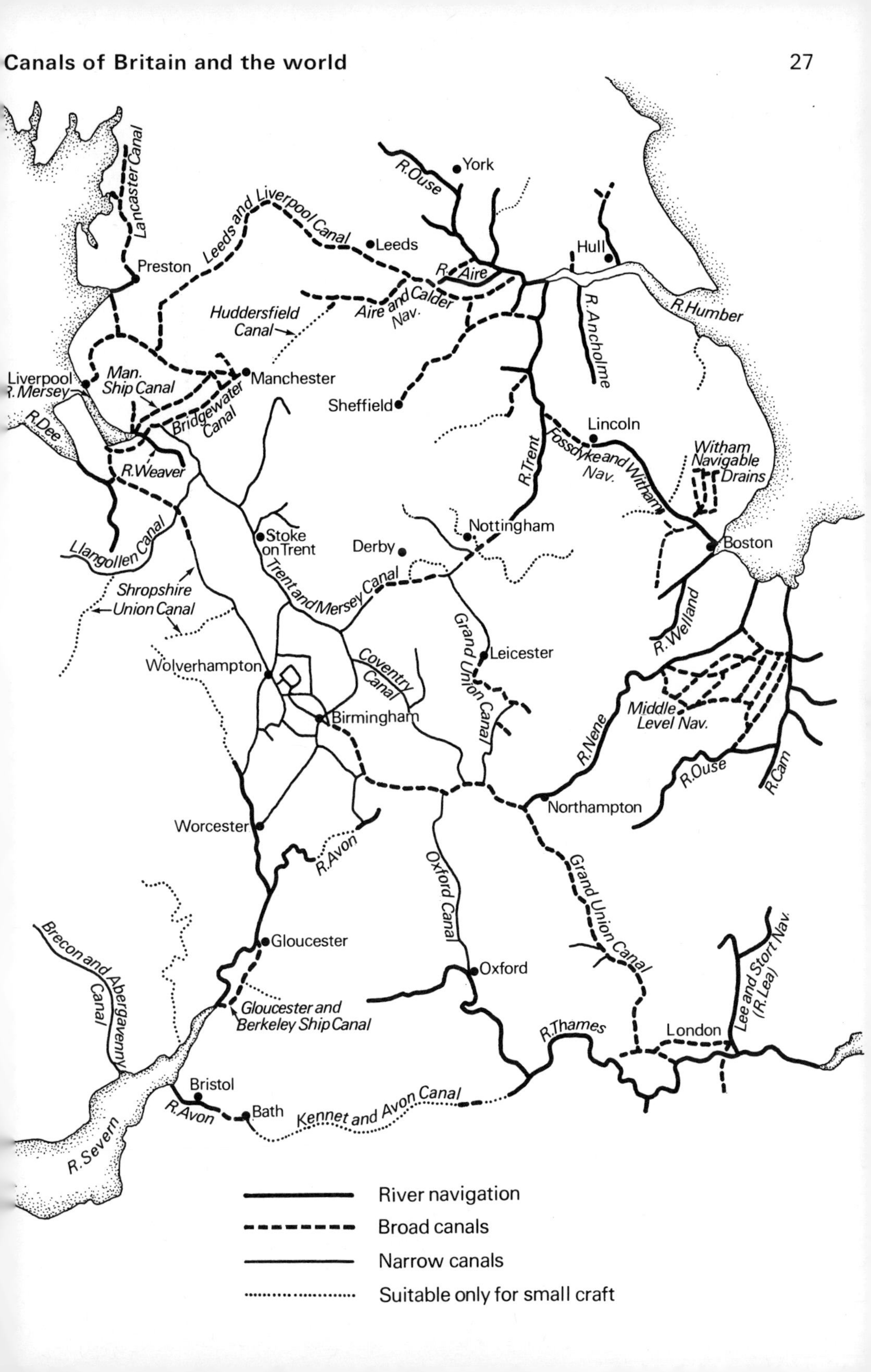
Lancaster Canal
York
R.Ouse
Leeds and Liverpool Canal
Leeds
Hull
Preston
R.Aire
Aire and Calder Nav.
R.Humber
Huddersfield Canal
R.Ancholme
Liverpool
R.Mersey
Man. Ship Canal
Manchester
Sheffield
R.Dee
Bridgewater Canal
Lincoln
R.Weaver
R.Trent
Fossdyke and Witham Nav.
Witham Navigable Drains
Nottingham
Llangollen Canal
Stoke on Trent
Derby
Boston
Trent and Mersey Canal
Shropshire Union Canal
R.Welland
Grand Union Canal
Leicester
Wolverhampton
Coventry Canal
Middle Level Nav.
Birmingham
R.Nene
R.Ouse
R.Cam
Northampton
Worcester
R.Avon
Oxford Canal
Grand Union Canal
Brecon and Abergavenny Canal
Gloucester
Lee and Stort Nav. (R.Lea)
Oxford
Gloucester and Berkeley Ship Canal
R.Thames
London
Bristol
R.Avon
Bath
Kennet and Avon Canal
R.Severn
River navigation
Broad canals
Narrow canals
Suitable only for small craft

boats (page 33) or pleasure craft. Most of the canals were nationalised in 1947 and most waterways have some government control (see page 66). It will be seen from the map that the canals link the heart of England with the four large rivers – Thames, Severn, Mersey and Humber. This system is sometimes called 'the cross'. Notice which large sea ports it connects.
You might like to find out more about the river navigations and canals which are shown on the map. You will find help for this in some of the books recommended on page 71.
Here are some suggestions of interesting things to look for:

1 Discover which canals are still used industrially. Which are the busiest from this point of view? Which are now most popular with holidaymakers?
2 Why have some remained open whilst others have closed? You may be able to find particular reasons for closures. Was it anything to do with railways? Roads?
3 Find out about the work of the Inland Waterways Association and of various canal trusts, such as the Kennet and Avon Canal Trust, which are at present working to keep open or re-open inland waterways.
4 Canal towns and ports such as Stourport grew up in the canal age. How have they been affected by canal changes?
5 Plan a journey 'along the cut' and note all that you would see that is of interest. Better still, make the journey yourself and take notes en route.

Whatever else your study includes, you should certainly find room for work on locks, bridges, tunnels, tow-paths, ironwork and canal buildings.
There are few canals in Scotland, the most important being the Caledonian Canal, which cuts across Scotland from Fort William to Inverness, the Crinan Canal, the Forth and Clyde Canal (closed 1963) and the Union Canal. The Aberdeenshire Canal closed over a century ago.

## Ship canals

Certain canals have been built to carry ocean-going ships. The most important of these in Britain is the Manchester Ship Canal which opened in 1894. This enables large cargo ships to reach

Manchester and has turned an inland city into an important port.
The Caledonian Canal and Crinan Canal, mentioned above, are also ship canals, and so is the Gloucester and Berkeley Ship Canal, but these can take only small ships.
Most ship canals provide a short cut to save a long journey. The Caledonian Canal, for example, saves a voyage right round the north of Scotland.
Ship canals in other parts of the world are much larger. For many years the Suez Canal was the most important. It linked the Mediterranean Sea and the Red Sea and shortened the route between Europe and the East. You might find out more about the canal, about Ferdinand de Lesseps who built it, about Britain's control of it for many years and why it is now closed. If it were to reopen would it be as important as it once was? Why? The Panama Canal through Central America is also very important as it saves a long and difficult voyage round the

*The Barton swing aqueduct and road bridge on the Manchester Ship Canal open to allow a ship to pass up to Manchester.*

stormy Cape Horn at the southern tip of South America.
The Kiel Canal in north Germany is a short cut from the North Sea to the Baltic and may be used by over two hundred ships in a single day. The Corinth Canal in Greece is too small for the large present-day cargo ships but smaller ones use the four-mile canal and so save a voyage of four hundred miles.
The Göta Canal which crosses Sweden from Gothenburg to Stockholm consists of rivers, lakes and canals. It was planned by Thomas Telford and was of particular value to the Swedes when Denmark controlled the entrance to the Baltic and charged dues on all ships passing through. The Göta Canal is used very little now for commercial ships, but passenger ships carry many people in summer along one of the most beautiful waterways in the world.
Another sea-to-sea canal is the Languedoc Canal in France, on which small ships can travel from the Mediterranean to the Bay of Biscay. It was a remarkable achievement when it was built in the seventeenth century. A much more recent achievement is the St Lawrence Seaway in North America (see page 44) by which ocean ships can reach the Great Lakes.
You might find these canals an interesting study. Perhaps you could add the many smaller canals in the Netherlands, Belgium, France and Germany. And what about the canal cities, such as Venice, Amsterdam and Stockholm in which canals take the place of streets in parts of the city? Can you discover why?
Look for maps which show the seas or towns which are linked by these various canals. Maps will be important in your own study, too, so make sure that you include them. You may try making a 3D model or you may feel that maps are quite suitable. You can use colours to show the different heights of ground. Some of your maps should be accurate: others need only be sketch maps. You may decide to use maps with pictures on them like those which are sometimes printed on holiday postcards.

## Canals and rivers in paintings

If you live in an industrial town, your canal or river may seem dull or dirty. Get outside the town and you will find, as many others have found, that it can be very beautiful. Look at the

'Venice: The Basin of S. Marco on Ascension Day' (by Canaletto, 1697–1768).

'Landscape with a Watermill' (by Boucher, 1703–70).

fine lines of the bridges, the colours of the sunset reflected in the water, reflections of trees and buildings, the ripples set up by the movement of boats or the fish which leaps to catch a fly. Think of the pattern of circles caused by raindrops. Do you think that you could capture some of these in pictures?

Many artists have found canals and rivers a source of inspiration. For some it was the natural feeling for the water that made it a choice of subject: for others the infinite variety of colour found in the damp atmosphere of the river. Yet others have been attracted by waterside buildings and boats, including, for example, the French artist, François Boucher (1703–70), who used the mill as the central subject, and Giovanni Antonio Canaletto (1697–1768), the Italian artist who painted many pictures of Venice, illustrating not only its beauty, but also the value of the gondola to the people of that city. Look for pictures by English painters. Constable, for example, painted many river scenes in oils and water colours and also made many pencil sketches.

Canals of the Netherlands also feature quite frequently in the works of Dutch artists. Here are some you could look for:

Meindert Hobbema (1638–1709) *The Herring-packers' Tower, Amsterdam*
Vincent Van Gogh (1853–90) *The Drawbridge*
Jan Vermeer (1632–65) *View of Delft*
Jacob van Ruysdael (1628–82) *Windmill at Wijk*

You might like to find out more about river and canal art. Get copies of pictures, decide whether you like the style of painting and find out a little about the artists.

Remember also the art of the canal people themselves, especially the paintings that adorned their narrow boats.

How about trying your own hand at painting river or canal scenes? You do not need to be an expert and you will probably not find it difficult to obtain advice from your art teacher or from others on the choice of subject and techniques of painting. Or, of course, you could try pencil, ink or charcoal sketching.

# Canal and river traffic 5

*Painted narrow boats*

*Broad boats, local craft, lighters and barges*

*Ships, ports and harbour craft*

Take a stroll along the canal bank and make a note of all the traffic you see. Among many kinds of boat you will probably see narrow boats like those in the picture on page 34. The main body of the boat is the cargo-carrying area covered by a raised tarpaulin, behind which is the cabin in which the canal folk live. Canal people have always been proud of their boats, decorating them with fancy ropework, brasses and paintings of castles and roses.

Canal boats like these often work in pairs. One, the 'motor boat', has an engine: the other, the 'butty boat' has to be towed. When under way the boatman may steer the motor boat and his wife the other. They steer with a large tiller attached to the rudder. Narrow boats were nearly always family boats with children living on board. Canal children could not go regularly to school but there are special arrangements for them now. See whether you can find out what they are.

You will realise why these boats are long and narrow. When Brindley planned the central section of the Trent and Mersey Canal he decided upon locks which were 74 ft long and 7 ft wide and so the boats were built just a little smaller – about 72 ft long and 6 ft 10 in. wide. On other canals sizes were a little different to suit the locks and tunnels. Boats which were to be carried up inclines (slopes) in cradles had to be much smaller.

The first boats, of course, had no engines for none had been invented. At first barges were 'bow hauled' up rivers by a gang of men hauling on a rope, which was fixed high up the mast to keep it clear of the bank along which the hauliers walked. In time their place was taken by horses which plodded along the tow-path, led often by a boy. There were certain rules on the canals about the age of the boy who led the horse. On some canals he had to be sixteen but on others he could be as young as ten. The rules also said that the boat should be steered by an able-bodied man over eighteen.

You might find it interesting to make a study of these early canal boats and their crews with any regulations or by-laws concerning them. You could also find out more about the hauliers and horses and the attitudes toward them of those whose land bordered the canal or river.

Some of the horses belonged to the boat owners: others, particularly on the river navigations could be hired and changed at various intervals. On the whole the horses were considered valuable and were well treated but some of the hired animals came in for some harsh treatment. On some canals narrow boats or barges were towed by one or two mules or donkeys.

Two horses were used to pull fast passenger boats which were called *fly boats* or *swift boats*. These were narrow boats which had very fine lines and little draught so that they could be pulled easily through the water. They had a cabin for passengers and also carried light goods. Two horses were harnessed 'in tandem' (one behind the other) with a rider or postilion on the

*Inland narrow boats on the Grand Union Canal at Gayton Junction, Northamptonshire.*

*Steamer on the Grand Junction Canal, in days gone by.*

second. They could pull the fly-boat at about eight to nine miles per hour and were changed at frequent intervals. These express boats were popular in days of bad roads before railways had developed. Fly-boats had the right of way over other traffic on the canal.
You might like to find out more about rules or 'by-laws' concerning right of way, the use of locks and mooring, such as these:

Loaded coal barges had right of way over empty ones. Why?
Distance posts to determine who should first use a lock.
Barges to be unhitched and manhandled into locks. Why?
No barge to be moored in a lock overnight.
No barge to be moored on the tow-path side.

These are just a few by-laws made for particular canals. They were not necessarily the same for all (see also page 66).
Great changes came to the canals when steam engines came into general use. Apart from steam tugs to assist boats through tunnels there were boats fitted with steam engines. These made life much easier for the canal people. Why did steamers give way to motor boats?

*Tugs and lighters on the Thames.*

## Broad boats and local craft

When thinking of canal craft it would be wrong to think only of the narrow boats. Many of the broad canals carried barges much larger than these. They are sometimes referred to as wide or broad boats and they are found on canals which join river navigations. Different kinds of craft are found on canals and rivers and these have developed according to local needs.

Most of the river craft originally had sails, though these gradually gave way to steam or motorized craft. The principal ones were the Severn trow, the Yorkshire keel, the Norfolk wherry, the Thames barge and the Mersey and Weaver flats. The Yorkshire keel was the last British craft to carry a square sail. The Norfolk wherry had an interesting balanced mast and rigging which could be lowered quickly when passing under low bridges. Unlike most river and canal craft, the wherry was not flat-bottomed.

The Thames barge had a fine spread of sail, yet was so designed that it could be handled by a crew of only two. It was a flat-bottomed vessel which could sit comfortably on the mud at low water. Since it had no keel, the Thames barge had a leeboard on either side which could be lowered when the barge was under sail. Only a few Thames barges remain under sail: others have had most of their rigging removed and a small engine fitted. If the wind failed, these local craft had either to remain becalmed or be moved by manpower. The Norfolk wherry, for example, was moved by means of a long pole or 'quant'. Similar poles or 'shafts' were used by boatmen when passing through tunnels which were unsuitable for 'legging'. Lightermen on the Thames are able, when necessary, to propel their craft with long oars or 'sweeps'.

How about collecting or drawing pictures of some of these local craft and writing a little about each? You could give dimensions, details of the trade in which they are used and a little information about their development.

You may perhaps see 'trains' of barges on rivers and canals. In the past, tugs used to tow trains of narrow boats through a tunnel. In the west of England trains of tub boats were developed. These were rectangular tubs which could be towed by a horse and kept in the centre of the waterway by means of a shaft operated from the tow-path. The modern development of the tub boat is the 'Tom Pudding' seen on the Aire and Calder Navigation in Yorkshire. As many as thirty of these coal-carrying tubs can be towed by one tug, though nineteen is the usual number for ease in passing through locks. A dummy bow is fitted to the leading tub and the train is towed to Goole where each tub can be lifted from the water and the coal emptied into ships.

On the larger waterways such as the Humber, Trent and Thames, larger craft may be seen, including barges which carry petroleum from the refineries to the inland towns. Mention has already been made of the lighters found on the Thames and along the Lee Navigation. These are 'swim-ended' craft. Perhaps you can find out what that means. They have no engines and are often seen on the Thames being towed in three pairs by small tugs. Look out for pictures of tugs. There are many different kinds – small motor tugs for river and canal work, larger ones for helping ships to their berths and very powerful ones for ocean rescue work.

Do you think you might also like to find out about inland waterway craft of Europe and America? Compare the size with that of British craft. Rhine barges (page 38) are much larger. On these waterways, too, it is not uncommon to find 'pusher' tugs and barges built for special purposes.

## Ports and sea-going vessels

As the rivers approach the sea, many different kinds of ship may be seen. Some are the small motor vessels like those in the picture on page 7 which trade coastwise or with the continent of Europe. They can reach some inland ports such as Norwich, Wisbech, Boston, Exeter and Gloucester which cannot be reached by larger ships.

Nearer the sea are the ports for big ships. Most of these ports have enclosed docks which are full of water even at low tide. To enter the dock a ship must use a lock similar to those on inland waterways but much larger.

You might be interested to find out more about the ships which use these ports and the cargoes they carry. You could also see whether any of this cargo is *transhipped* – loaded into smaller craft to be carried up-river.

## Harbour craft

In the port area there are many kinds of craft to be seen – launches, floating cranes, water boats, fire floats, lifeboats and others. Then there are dredgers of various kinds necessary for keeping the fairway clear of the silt or 'spoil' carried down the river. Dredgers of course may also be seen in other parts of the

*Cargo is transhipped from ships to Rhine barges at Rotterdam.*

*Grab-hopper dredger working near docks entrance, London.*

river together with other boats used by the river authority to make sure that the river remains open to those boats or ships which will use it, including holiday boats which are now found on most waterways (see chapter 7).

There are other river and canal craft which you might like to find out about for yourself. Here are some:

Water buses and passenger service launches
Passenger and car ferries
Sludge vessels and hopper barges
'Puffers' and small motor vessels on Scottish canals
Maintenance craft and ice-breakers on canals
Fishing boats

On overseas waterways:

Lake freighters on the St Lawrence Seaway, Canada
Special barges on rivers in the USA
Rhine and Danube barges
Feluccas and other native craft
Excursion or holiday vessels on the Rhine or Göta Canal
Stern-wheel paddlers (historical)

# 6 Waterways and industry

*Waterways as transport links*

*Water power for mills and power stations*

*Reservoirs, water works and riverside industries*

You will not have to look far along a river or the industrial part of a canal to find various industries which depend upon the water for carrying goods or, in the case of rivers, for power. Make a survey in your area and see how many there are.
We have touched briefly on the question of transport already. It was for this reason that Brindley built the Bridgewater Canal and sparked off the desire for canals by industrialists in other parts of the country. You might find it worth while to discover what industries they were which needed canal transport in the eighteenth century.
Rivers also served some industries. Norfolk wherries carried large quantities of sugar beet to the factories. Raw materials were carried upstream to factories and manufactured goods downstream for export. Industries, which could use the coal transported in narrow boats and barges from the coalfields, were established near the waterways.
Nowadays you may find depots for oil instead of coal and new factories that have replaced the old ones. Talk to someone who works in them and find out why they need the waterway.

## Water power

Water is a useful source of power which has been known for a very long time. The Greeks used water wheels and the Romans made good use of that invention. In Britain, water wheels drove the mills which ground corn for the abbey or the manor and many of these are listed in the Domesday Book.
There are two kinds of water wheel. An *overshot* wheel is one

*The riverside mill at St Ives, built in 1854–6, was a steam flour mill drawing water from the river and one of the finest mills of its day. Later it became a paper mill and is now a factory.*

used where the water tumbles down hill and across the top of the wheel, pushing the blades of the wheel forward as it does so. The *undershot* wheel is one in which the lower part of the wheel is in the water and pushed by the stream (see page 31).

Often a water mill is built just off the main river, which is dammed so that water is diverted through a mill race at a much faster speed than the river flows. You can appreciate why the millers were often unwilling to allow the staunches to be opened to river craft when this meant loss of power for their mills. There are still some water mills working. If you can see one, notice how it works, perhaps drawing a sketch of the gears and millstones and explaining how the grain is fed to the millstones. Mills, in their picturesque setting of mill race or mill pool, make an attractive subject for painting or sketching.

In the eighteenth century, water came to be used for driving the machinery of a different kind of mill. Water was used by Richard Arkwright to provide power for his 'water frame' in the mills at Cromford and later in other mills in the textile industry. This was an early part of the Industrial Revolution. You could find out more about this and the important part played by rivers and canals.

Water wheels were used before this in the sixteenth century iron industry, to give power to bellows and forge hammers. These heavy hammers were lifted by a cam on the shaft of the wheel, then dropped onto the hot iron on an anvil.

Another industry which used hammers was that of paper-making. In the eighteenth century paper was made from rags which were pounded into pulp in paper mills by a series of hammers on a shaft. Nowadays pulp and paper mills are still found by rivers but for a somewhat different reason. Most paper today is made from wood. Softwoods are taken to the pulp mills where the wood is chipped and the fibres separated either by chemical processing or by grinding. In either case the product is a slushy mixture known as pulp. For some papers the pulp may also contain fibres of grass, cotton rag or linen and china clay for whitening. The pulp then goes to the paper mills, where it passes over and under rollers until it emerges as rolls of paper. The modern pulp and paper mills are driven by electricity but a vast amount of water is needed for both processes.

Apart from this, the river provides the means by which the logs reach the pulp mill. Rivers are especially noted for this ir Canada, where logs are stacked on the frozen rivers then carriec down by the surge of water at the time of the spring thaw You may have seen pictures of lumberjacks riding the logs o of tugs towing thousands of logs in a 'boom' to the mills.

This brief introduction to an important industry may lead you to look more closely into paper making or possibly into the timber industry too, for this also depends on water transport.

### Electricity

Most of the factories and mills along the riverside are nov powered by electricity. But rivers play a vital role in the makin of most electricity.

Most of the large power stations are built by rivers. Electricit is made by huge generators, some of which are driven by stean and receive their coal supplies by river. Some of this coal i taken direct from the colliers at the power station: some ma be taken in barges by river or canal. If the generators are drive by steam power a large quantity of water is needed and thi must be taken from a river. Look upstream of the power station for an inlet channel: look downstream and you will see where the water flows out. Where the water supply is limited, as on small rivers, look for large curved cooling towers in which the water is cooled for further use. From the power station electricity may be carried across the river by cables on pylons to the consumer.

*Paper mill at Northfleet, Kent, showing pulp stacking area (left) and the machine houses and power station (right).*

*Thorpe Marsh power station, Yorkshire. Notice the cooling towers, necessary as this is not a large river.*

*Beauharnois power dam and locks on the St Lawrence Seaway, Canada.*

Another source of electricity is that known as hydro-electricity. In this case the generators are driven by water power. This is a method frequently used in mountainous country such as the highlands of Scotland where there are fast-flowing streams and rivers.

The principle is similar to that of the water mill. A large volume of water is directed through a small channel so that it has tremendous force behind it. You could find out more about making electricity (see page 72). You might also discover how the water supply to power stations and mills can be 'cut off' when not required. The river does not stop flowing. One of the requirements for hydro-electricity is a dam to hold back the water. When the St Lawrence Seaway in Canada was constructed, dams formed an important part of the work so that hydro-electric power stations could be provided.

Several famous dams have been constructed in recent years including the Kariba Dam on the Zambezi in Central Africa, the Aswan Dam on the Nile in Egypt and the Tennessee Valley dams in the USA.
You might like to consider the uses of dams to industry and agriculture.

## Reservoirs and water works

Large quantities of water must be provided for factories that are far from rivers and also for home use. Have you ever tried to work out how much water you use in a day? This water has to be treated before it can be used so that it is fit for drinking or cooking. You could perhaps arrange a visit to a waterworks to see a pumping station and filter beds. Water for the water-works is stored in reservoirs, which are man-made lakes. Some are formed by damming a river valley and perhaps 'drowning' a village as the water rises in the reservoir. Discuss with your friends whether you think this should be done. City people must have water. But should valleys be drowned to provide it?
In the picture on page 46, you can see reservoirs in the Lea Valley which supply part of London with water. See how the centre of the valley has been built up to form these huge tanks of water. The original course of the river has disappeared and a waterway for barge traffic can be seen on the left with a lock abreast the reservoir. River channels also pass on the other side.
Which rivers contribute to your water supply?

## Other industries

Along the banks of a river are other industries which are there because of the river.
It is natural, for example, that there should be places at which boats and ships can be built and repaired. Boatyards are found on most rivers and canals. Some build mainly the business craft of the waterway: others concentrate more on holiday or pleasure craft, or on small boats used by local fishermen. There are also shipyards at which ocean liners can be built.

*Lea Valley reservoirs at Chingford, Essex. The Lee Navigation (constructed) is on the left. A lock can be seen beside the reservoir. Channels on the right feed the waterworks or act as overflows. (The spelling Lea is used for the river but Lee for the navigation.)*

*Boatyard beside the river at Wivenhoe, Essex.*

See whether you can find a boatyard or shipyard and find out more for yourself about these industries. How are boats and ships built? Of what materials?

You might also see whether there are any local fisheries such as salmon or shellfish, or possibly a fish farm from which rivers can be restocked.

Can you find other industries or public services? Warehousing? Wharfage? Sewage farms? Others?

# 7 Waterways for pleasure

*River and canal holidays*

*Excursions and boating activities*

*Fishing and other riverside pleasures*

'There is nothing – absolutely nothing – half so much worth doing as simply messing about in boats! . . .' So said Rat to his new friend Mole in *The Wind in the Willows*. He was voicing a feeling that has been echoed by many people who have found great enjoyment on rivers and canals simply messing around in boats. It is a pleasant way of relaxing or of travelling slowly in contrast to the bustle and rush of every day to which so many people are accustomed.

If your nearest waterway is used by pleasure boats, spend a morning or an afternoon by the water and make a survey of all the boats that pass. This will have to be during the summer because most pleasure boats are only insured for summer use and are 'laid up' during the winter. Why do you think this is so? Make notes about each boat that passes – the name of the boat, what kind it is, its colour, its size and the number of people you can see on board. You could also see whether it is built of wood, metal or fibreglass, whether it looks like an old lifeboat that has been converted, and whether it carries the badge of a company that hires out boats. There are hire companies on most rivers and canals.

Instead of waiting on the bank for boats to pass, you could go to one of the places where many boats are often seen. There are popular moorings on some waterways and there are places where people can leave their boats in winter or during the week if they want them mainly at week-ends. A place like this is called a 'marina' or 'boat haven'. You would need to ask for permission to look around one of these. Look for the moorings, a slipway up which boats can be taken for repair, a workshop

pumps for petrol and diesel oil, and a shop in which all sorts of gear can be bought.
You will probably also find boats moored at the town quay (see the picture on page 13), where there may be a tap for drinking water and dustbins for rubbish (which should *never* be dropped overboard). At any of these places you may be able to chat to boat owners about their boats. They might possibly be willing to show you what the boat is like inside.
If you cannot do this, look for a boat in a boatyard or at a boat show. You will soon notice how much is built into a very small space. Why do you think this is? How would you plan a boat that would be suitable for yourself and your family?
Some people like to keep close to their marinas or boat havens but others cruise on longer journeys. There are many places where you can moor to the banks at meal times or for the night. You have to obey any local rules about mooring and also remember that some river banks are private property.
It is from moorings like this that you can sit quietly to enjoy the world of nature. You may be visited by cows, which can be very inquisitive creatures. What kind of things would you hear or notice early in the morning? At mid-day? At sunset? Go along to your river or canal bank and find out. If you have ever had a holiday on a river or canal you could no doubt make a list of the 'dos and don'ts' of boating. The main thing to remember is that one can never be in a hurry but must have patience and show courtesy and consideration to others. You can find out much about boating from the Waterways series of books (see page 71).
For those who are not as energetic but who would enjoy a canal holiday with the boat run by professionals, there are canal hotel boats on which one can enjoy canal cruising without having to cook, wash up or clamber ashore to work locks. It is also possible to enjoy day or short excursions on some of the waterways. Steamers and motor launches run regular services on the Thames from Oxford down to Greenwich; waterbuses operate on the Grand Union Canal in London; and excursion boats are found on many other rivers and canals. There are many who enjoy days on the river in boats which are too small to sleep in, many having outboard motors. Yet other people prefer to stay put and have houseboats at the riverside.

*A sailing race on the Norfolk Broads.*

Canals, on the whole are suitable only for engined or towed boats. Rivers, because of their width and other features, can be used by sailing boats. A sailing boat has the disadvantage that it cannot sail a straight course but must 'tack' back and forth in a zig-zag manner. The boats most commonly seen on rivers are dinghies – small boats with two sails – though larger boats may be seen in estuaries.

There are those, too, who like the hard work of rowing or sculling. (What is the difference?) Well-known events like the University Boat Race and the Henley Regatta are only two occasions when 'racing eights' take to the water. Canoes too may be seen in many places, especially where rapids or other dangers make the canoeing more exciting.

Perhaps you would like to write about boating activities of many kinds on rivers and canals.

## Fishing

Others who get a great amount of pleasure from our waterways are fishermen or, to give them their correct name, anglers. They are often found singly or in groups sitting on the river bank with their gear set out, their lines cast, and waiting patiently for a bite. Sometimes they may be sitting in punts or on cabin cruisers or, for certain kinds of fish, wading in the river.

Many sections of river bank are reserved for members of angling clubs, who may have a long journey to reach that particular river. Are you keen on fishing? If not, perhaps you have a relative who is. If so you will know that fishermen are not put off by bad weather and they may often be seen in waterproof clothing beneath large umbrellas in weather which would keep most people cooped up indoors.

You might like to make a list of what gear is necessary for fishing in your local water. What kind of fish can be caught there? (See page 58). What would local people think to be a good catch? Talk about this to someone who is keen on fishing. You could find out from him what conditions are best for catching those fish and what equipment is needed. Is one rod and line enough? Or should you have more?

You might also talk about the bait to be used – ground bait, live bait, artificial lures, and so on. It is no use having the equipment if you cannot persuade the fish to bite.

The majority of the fish caught in rivers are known as *coarse* fish. These may not be caught at certain times of the year. See if you can find out when this 'close' season is. There are also rules regarding the size of fish which may be taken and which must be returned to the water. Discuss with your fishing friend why these rules are made and find out any other rules or 'by-laws' which apply to your local river, including the matter of fishing licences.

Fly fishing is the method of catching 'game' fish like salmon and trout. This is only possible in some rivers and only in the 'open' season.

## Riverside inns and gardens

Some people simply wish to relax by the river, to sit on the bank or in riverside inns, restaurants or gardens and watch the river flow by. Many of the inns are those which date back long before the days of pleasure boating. Most have names which speak of the water – 'The Ferry Boat', 'The Pike and Eel', 'The Lock', 'The Wharf Tavern'. It might be interesting for you to find out which public houses or inns stand by your nearest waterway, discover a little of their history and why they are so named.

You must obviously have some feeling for rivers or canals to choose this as a subject. What kinds of pleasure do you get from them?

# Wild life of rivers and canals 8

*Looking for wild life on rivers and canals*

*Introduction to birds, mammals, amphibians and fish*

*Plants and trees of the river bank*

One thing that attracts many people to our waterways is the variety of animal and plant life to be seen. A river or canal is the home of many kinds of fish: its banks house various animals and provide nesting places for birds. Both in and out of the water there is abundant plant life.

The kind of thing to be seen will obviously vary from place to place but some are common to most waterways. You might like to take a walk along the banks of your nearest one, or perhaps go and just sit for a while, for many wild creatures are shy of moving people. Preferably do this in late spring or summer when there are more creatures to be seen.

Perhaps you will notice the insects first for there are so many of them and they are less fearful of people than are animals and birds. There are flies which seem often to be attracted to people and animals. Beautiful dragonflies may sometimes be seen over the water in which they have spent the larva period of their lives. Keep an eye open for the more brightly coloured flies which are seldom seen in town. There are many small creatures too – beetles, spiders and lots of others. Perhaps you could try to identify any you do not know. Some you will know already. The wasp that wishes to share your food and the gnats and midges which you encounter in the evenings are not the most welcome of insects.

But if midges and gnats are unpopular with people, they are welcomed by the swallows and sand-martins which can be seen swooping over the water in the evening, catching insects on the wing. Fish also leap out of the water to catch low-flying insects.

*A heron resting by the water. When watching for fish his long neck will be extended.*

## Birds

Some birds which are seen on waterways are very well known for they are also found frequently on lakes and ponds. Swans and ducks can make themselves at home in many places. Swans are perhaps at their most interesting when the young cygnets are born and when the parent birds proudly swim with their offspring in a single line behind. Swans at this stage are very protective and should be approached with caution.

Mallards, like many birds, are at their best in springtime, when the drakes have their brightest plumage to attract their mates.

Mallards are the commonest but not the only kind of ducks to be seen on rivers. One may also see domestic ducks and geese belonging to local people.
Where there are banks with reeds, sedges or overhanging trees there are also likely to be moorhens and coots. The moorhen, which has a red base to its bill and black plumage with white under the tail is a shy bird which darts for cover. Moorhens often swim across the water a little ahead of oncoming boats. Coots, which are larger than moorhens, have white beaks which extend into a frontal shield.
One large bird that may be seen by the water is the heron, a grey wading bird which stands perfectly still until an unwary fish passes nearby. Herons are more frequently seen in the flatter parts of the country and in side waters. They nest in trees near the water. The heron will take off when approached but settle again not far away.
Some birds, notably the grebes and the divers, disappear under the water whenever a boat approaches, then surface some distance away. They are found mainly in reedy areas. The Great Crested Grebe has a long neck and in summer, tufts on its head. It has a most interesting courtship display. The Black-throated Diver and Red-throated Diver are sometimes seen on rivers and lakes. Occasionally a kingfisher may be seen. These small beautiful brightly-coloured birds wait on branches for fish to pass beneath, then plunge in a flash of colour to seize the fish. They nest in the river bank in chambers leading from small tunnels which they excavate.
In the plants at the river's edge are small birds like the Sedge Warbler, Reed Warbler and Reed Bunting: in marshy places wagtails, lapwing and plover. Gulls are also found on inland waters. You could make a study of these birds, finding out about colouring, size, nesting habits, eggs, food and migration. You might also consider birds found in foreign rivers or estuaries, such as pelicans, flamingos, egrets and other species of swans, ducks and geese.

**Mammals, amphibians and reptiles**

There are several small mammals which inhabit British rivers and canals, the largest of them being the otter. This is a flesh

*A water shrew.*

eating animal which feeds mainly on fish. It lives in hollow trees, between roots or in similar places where it can hide away. Otters may also travel long distances over land. They are animals which move at night and are therefore seldom seen.

On some rivers, particularly in East Anglia, coypus may be found. These rodents were originally brought from South America for fur farming but a few escaped and bred along the rivers. A smaller rodent is the water vole, which also lives in holes in the river bank and may sometimes be seen swimming near the bank.

The smallest of our water mammals is the water shrew, a tiny black and white animal which seldom moves far from the water and builds its nest in a small tunnel.

Do not expect to see any of these animals. You may be fortunate enough to do so if you keep very still and are in the right place at the right time. You will probably have to content yourself with finding out about them and examining the holes in the

*Look for any holes in the river bank.*

river bank which may have been made by them.
You may be able to find amphibians (frogs, toads and newts) nearby but these are more frequently found in still waters.
If you are including mammals and reptiles of foreign rivers, you will be able to find many that are more exciting or more interesting to watch than the British ones. Here are some:

Hippopotamus alligator crocodile water buffalo
beaver river hog salamander water snakes (e.g. anaconda)

**Fish**

Many kinds of fish are to be found in British waterways, depending upon the nature of the water. Some prefer the upper parts of the river where they can dart quickly through the tumbling waters. Some prefer the slower-moving waters where they can remain out of sight or move amongst the water plants. Yet others live equally well in salt or fresh water and often inhabit the waters of an estuary.
Most of these fish feed on vegetable matter, small insects, snails and tiny fish but some are predatory, that is they feed on other fish. The pike is the most vicious of our freshwater fish and has sharp teeth. It is sometimes called the freshwater shark.

If you would like to find out more about some of these fish, here is a very rough guide.

*In shallow or fast-running brooks*
Bleak bullhead dace grayling loach minnow stickleback

*Generally in deeper or slow-moving waters*
Barbel bream carp chub gudgeon perch pike roach rudd tench (also minnows and sticklebacks)

*In estuaries*
Bass flounder grey mullet (also shellfish)

Salmon, trout and eels are fish which travel. Perhaps you could find out for yourself about the remarkable journeyings of eels which cross the Atlantic to breed and of salmon which are able to leap up waterfalls.
Some fish are more easily seen than others. Make sure that your shadow does not fall on the water but look in clear waters from a bridge, or along the walls of a lock, or perhaps near waterlily leaves.

## Plant life

The plant life of rivers and canals can be divided roughly into

*Waterlilies.*

*A familiar riverside tree is the White Willow (left). The ornamental Weeping Willow (right) often found by rivers originated in China.*

wo – plants which grow in the water and plants which grow eside the water. Flowering plants like waterlilies and various vater weeds which spread rapidly, grow in the water.

lear the banks on slowly-flowing rivers one may frequently nd clusters of plants belonging to the sedge family. These are ll sedges and rushes (pictured on page 14), having a single tem from which broad leaves grow. Many have pinkish or rown flowers and feathery seed heads. There are also clusters f reedmace with their brown sausage-shaped close-set female owers often mistakenly called bulrushes. The true bulrush is a ember of the sedge family.

n the banks are many kinds of flower which add colour to e scene. Some of these are mainly riverside plants but others so grow in other places. Here are some you might like to find ut about. Add any others that you find yourself.

urple loosestrife yellow loosestrife comfrey
dy's smock willowherb wild teasel
arsh marigold (kingcup) yellow flag (iris)
ater forget-me-not

A study of riverside flowers may take a long time as the flowers bloom at different times of year. You could pick and press some of the flowers but do not uproot any. Some plants are protected and it is forbidden to uproot them. In any case there are others who would like to enjoy them after you have left.

**Trees**

Willows and osiers are probably the most common trees which grow by rivers. There are various trees and shrubs in this family, for example, the White Willow and the Weeping Willow and they grow very close to the water with their roots running into the river bed. Some even stand in the water because the bank on which they once grew has been washed away.

Many of our national trees grow by the water and you might like to collect the leaves of any you find, then see how many you can identify. You could also make a count to find out which are the commonest or perhaps plot their positions by the river. Rivers and canals in Britain are seldom lined with trees for long before running into the open country again. How about comparing British rivers in this respect with tropical rivers like the Amazon or the Congo which flow through dense jungle or with those of Canada or Norway lined with coniferous trees?

# Conservation and control 9

*Controlling the water with sluices and flood barriers*

*Pollution, preservation and reclamation*

*River and canal authorities: by-laws and rights*

So far we have seen how useful rivers can be but there are times when they can bring disaster to those who live beside hem. The height of a river depends upon the amount of rain that falls to make the springs and feed the tributaries. It can be very dangerous if much more rain falls than usual. Rivers cannot contain all the extra water and then they overflow. Another danger is in spring when the snow melts and fills the streams which cascade down the hillsides to swell the river. A third danger comes from the other end of the river when unusually high tides flood in, holding back the river water so that it must overflow its banks.
Keep your eyes open for reports of floods and see whether you can find out why they happened. If the floods are near you, go and look for yourself. Find out how much higher than usual the ver water is, where it broke its banks and what damage has een done. Often people are taken unawares because some freak of nature causes floods where they have been unknown efore. In an area that has been flooded, look for flood marks n buildings.
n other places, floods are expected at certain periods and precautions are taken. A special watch is kept after heavy rain r snow or when the highest tides are expected.

## Sluices and flood barriers

Where floods are expected, it is common to find embankments f raised ground on either side of the river so that water would need to rise several feet before causing damage to property or

*A weir to control the water level and a lock with a guillotine gate (left) to allow boats to pass the weir.*

crops. Where danger from the sea exists it is sometimes possibl
to build a barrier to prevent the sea from flowing in. This wa
tackled on the Great Ouse in the fens as long ago as th
seventeenth century, when Dutch engineers under Corneliu
Vermuyden built the first great sluice at Denver.

This held back the tide but it also meant that there was n
longer the flood tide to provide enough water for navigation
Weirs had therefore to be built to control the water, wit
staunches (now locks) to allow craft to pass. The guillotin
lock gate found here owes its origin to the same period. It wa
the type used by the Dutch engineers.

For many years there has been discussion about the need for
huge barrier across the Thames to prevent flooding by hig
tides. Records kept since 1791 show that the danger is in
creasing. It is proposed that a barrier should be built acros
Woolwich Reach. This will consist of a series of concrete pier
containing machinery to operate the flood barriers which wi
normally lie out of sight below the river.

The Thames barrier is not intended to prevent the flow of th
river, so locks will not be necessary. But if a high tide surge
up the river, the barrier can be closed in a matter of minute
The design of this barrier is such that it will not interfere wit
the free movement of shipping except at danger periods. Thi

*Flooding on the River Nene at Duston Mill, Northamptonshire.*

is a very important consideration on a busy river like the Thames.

Perhaps you could find out more about barrages, sluices, weirs and other forms of river control.

You could also find out whether your local river is likely to be affected by flooding. Do you know of any precautions? Can you find any embankments? Are canals affected by flooding?

## Pollution

People have long been concerned at the way in which rivers can spoil or damage property on their banks. It is only recently that people have shown as much concern for the ways in which people can spoil rivers. This we call *pollution*. It means simply that so much waste and filth is pumped into rivers that they smell, they look unsightly and they kill off fish and other creatures.

Much of this is caused by the factories which use the river water and put back into the river much more than they take out – such things as oil, chemicals and detergents. Then there are the sewage farms. You can see one on the left of the photograph on page 46. Here in the filter beds the sewage is broken down by means of detergents and the resulting *effluence* is pumped into the river. Sometimes the detergent can form a coating of froth on the river but many would feel that this is preferable to the other practice of pumping raw sewage into the rivers which then become open sewers, unpleasant to sight and smell and a danger to health.

In 1971 the Government received a 'shocking' report on the state of rivers, canals and estuaries which showed that nearly one thousand miles of waterways were very polluted and over a thousand more were poor. A massive plan costing hundreds of millions of pounds was announced. It was a welcome scheme to clean up the waterways and one which was long overdue.

In certain areas where action has been taken, rivers are beginning to come back to life. Fish are swimming where they have not swum for years and the rivers are generally much more pleasant for those who use them.

The poisoning of fish has been only one aspect of the damage to wild life. Many a bird has died after being smothered in oil from a leaking barge and there are some rivers so bad that anyone falling in needs to be taken to hospital for examination. The cleansing of these rivers and canals, especially in the industrial north of England and Midlands is something that cannot be done too quickly.

You might like to find out more about the problems of pollution, its causes and its effects. What can be done to prevent it? Perhaps you could design posters to draw attention to the need for more thought.

Remember, too, that this is a matter for individuals as well as for factory bosses. You will not look far in rivers or canals before finding floating rubbish. And for all that floats there is much more that goes straight to the bottom. The river or canal, especially in town, seems to become the dumping place for almost anything. How about cleaning up an area as part of your project? If you do, be very careful for your safety.

### Preservation and reclamation

It is not just the water that needs to be protected. There are many buildings and pieces of equipment along our waterways that are of historical or architectural value. There is always a

*Rubbish is often dumped in rivers.*

danger that the old becomes lost as newer and more efficient things appear. Many canals were closed and lost as railways and roads improved. You might try to discover how railways affected the canals. Beside the canals were huge pumping engines, a few of which have fortunately been preserved. Would it interest you to find out more about these engines – the Newcomen type and the Boulton and Watt beam engines – and the purposes for which they were built?

Buildings, too, are worth preserving and some are now safe because of their especial interest value. Recently whole areas have come under control so that local historical features can be retained. Are there any on your waterway?

Some features of canals have also been preserved in museums, of which the most interesting must be the Waterways Museum, Stoke Bruerne, Northants (see page 72). Here may be seen many exhibits of a bygone age.

Important work is being done to preserve canals and canal history on the canals themselves. We have already seen how the Inland Waterways Association and the various canal trusts are trying to preserve existing waterways and to reclaim some of those which are at present unusable. It is a slow process which depends upon the amount of money which can be raised.

Sometimes good use can be made of equipment that is no longer needed elsewhere. Recently for example, lock gates from the blocked-off Grand Surrey Canal were given by the Port of London Authority to the Upper Avon Navigation Trust for use at Stratford-on-Avon. The Trust has been able to build several locks using gates presented by a number of waterway authorities. Perhaps you could look into the work that is being done today in preserving the old and reclaiming the disused.

### River and canal authorities

All waterways must have a body of people who are responsible for them. In recent years most canals and some river navigations have been controlled by the British Waterways Board: others like the Manchester Ship Canal and Bridgewater Canal by private companies. Rivers have for many years been controlled by river authorities or conservancy boards, responsible for one river or for all rivers in a particular area.

This will change. The Government has said that by 1974 there will be nine large river authorities which should be better able to clean up the waterways. Has this happened yet? Who controls your local rivers? Perhaps you can name other authorities too. You might be interested to find out more about the work that is done by these river and canal authorities and especially those who control your local waterways.

You could also look for old posters which give warnings to those who misused waterways in the past.

### Rights and regulations

One important part of the work of river authorities is the making of rules to protect the interests of all who use the river. There are those, for example, whose lands run down to the river.

# PUBLIC APOLOGY.

## LANCASTER CANAL.

I, the undersigned, THOMAS HENRY BURROW, late of Ellel, now of Gleestone, near Ulverstone, Farm Labourer, acknowledge and confess that on Monday Evening, the 8th of March, 1886, I wantonly and foolishly opened a Clough in a Lockgate in Glasson Lockage, which resulted in a waste of water, and for such offence have rendered myself liable to a penalty of Five Pounds, or not less than Forty Shillings, and in default of the payment of the Penalty, to imprisonment in the House of Correction for not exceeding Six Months nor less than Three Months; I now therefore

**PUBLICLY APOLOGIZE**

for such offence, and promise that I will not offend again; I request and hope that the Canal Proprietors will not prosecute me; and I authorize the printing and publication hereof at my cost and expense.

Dated this Sixteenth day of March, 1886.

**T. H. BURROW.**

E. & J. L. Milner, Guardian Printing Works, Lancaster. W/C3/5

*Public apology for misusing a canal.*

Some are farmers: others are house owners. They may wish to use water from the river or strengthen the river bank to protect their property. Certain angling clubs have the sole rights of fishing from the banks. Rights to use the river bank are known as *riparian* rights. Can you find out why?

We have already seen that there are rules which say when people can fish and what kind of fish they can take from the river. You could find out about by-laws which concern other river users. If there is not a copy of these in your public library, the librarian could probably tell you where to see one.

Boat owners must pay a fee and have their boats registered but they must also obey certain rules when on the river. Speed limits are necessary because boats travelling fast can wear away the banks. There are also certain safety rules to be observed. Spend half a day by the river and see what you notice about such things as right of way, which boats must give way and how to avoid a collision. In the lower reaches too where shipping is to be found there are navigational aids such as buoys and lights and these are shaped and coloured according to a scheme which is common to all British ports and coastal waters. You could perhaps find out more about buoys and other aids to shipping.

Other rules or by-laws concern mooring, damage, trespass, dangerous cargoes, water skiing, pollution, correct use of locks, and a whole host of other matters. They are made to safeguard the waterway and those who use it.

*A constable of Thames Division of the Metropolitan Police boarding a ship to give assistance to an injured dock worker.*

If there are regulations there must be those who make sure that they are kept. Many river authorities have wardens or water bailiffs to see to this. Some have launches in which officials can patrol and keep a general eye on what is happening. Larger rivers have police launches in which river police can patrol to keep law and order and to look into problems or dangers.

Many people are concerned with our waterways, some to look after them and others to use them. You might like to note the responsibilities of each for making and keeping rivers and canals as waterways that are a pleasure to see and to use.

# Some useful waterway words

*aqueduct* — a bridge carrying water.
*backwater* — branch off a main river.
*balance beam* — heavy beam attached to a lock gate.
*barge* — a flat-bottomed cargo boat over 7 ft wide, with or without an engine.
*butty* — narrow boat without an engine.
*canal* — a man-made waterway.
*cut* — the course of a canal.
*draught* — depth of a boat below water level.
*estuary* — a wide mouth of a river or rivers.
*flight* — a staircase of locks.
*ford* — shallow place where a river can be crossed.
*lock* — a basin of water enclosed between gates.
*mitre gates* — a pair of lock gates which meet pointing a little up-stream.
*navigation* — when applied to rivers, a river suitable for use by ships or barges.
*paddles* — sliding covers which allow water to enter a lock when opened.
*pound* — a lock or other enclosed water, e.g. the stretch between locks on a canal.
*reach* — a stretch of river, e.g. between locks or between bends.
*riparian* — to do with the river bank.
*side pond* — a small reservoir into which water can flow in a staircase of locks.
*slackers* — see 'paddles'.
*staunch* — a barrier and rising gate for holding back river water.
*towpath* — path beside a river or canal used by horses when towing barges.
*water bailiff* — an official employed to uphold by-laws.
*weir* — a barrier or dam across a river.

# Sources of information

There are many books on rivers and canals which you will find useful. Here is just a small selection.

Bethers, R., *Rivers of Adventure*, Constable, 1960.
Calvert, R., *Inland Waterways of Britain*, Ian Allan, 1963.
de Maré, E., *Your Book of Waterways*, Faber, 1965.
Hadfield, C., *British Canals*, David & Charles, 1950.
Hadfield, C., *Canals of the World*, Blackwell, 1964.
Hadfield, C., *The Canal Age*, David & Charles, 1968.
Jones, E., *The World of Water*, Blandford, 1969.
Metcalf, L., *Discovering Bridges*, Shire, 1970.
Metcalf, L., and Vince, J., *Discovering Canals*, Shire, 1968.
Murphy, J. S., *How they were Built: Canals*, Oxford, 1961.
Pilkington, R., *Boats over Land*, Abelard-Schuman, 1962.
Purton, R. W., *Ports and Sea Transport*, Blandford, 1972.
Rolt, L. T. C., *Navigable Waterways*, Longmans, 1969.
Ross, A., *Canals in Britain*, Blackwell, 1962.
Vince, J., *River and Canal Transport*, Blandford, 1970.
Wynward, J., *Dams and Canals*, Wheaton, 1964.

Apart from the general books mentioned above, regional canal books are published by David & Charles.
There is a folder of booklets and cards, Trailblazer 2: *Rivers* by R. E. Brett (1969), published by Thomas Nelson (formerly by Hamish Hamilton).
A very useful series of books about rivers and canals is the *Waterways Series*, published by Link House. These are *The Canals Book*, *The Thames Book*, and *The Broads Book* of which a revised edition is published each year. A fourth book, *The Fens Book* was published in a 1969 edition but you could ask your bookseller whether there is a later edition. *The Canals Book* gives information also about Canal Trusts.

For information about rivers and canals controlled by the *British Waterways Board*, write to The Enquiry Office, British Water-

ways Board, Melbury House, Melbury Terrace, London NW1. (Information can only be supplied on waterways controlled by the Board. This excludes the Thames and anything south of it, waterways east of the Lea and in East Anglia, and anything in England north of Yorkshire. It does include Scottish canals.)
The *Inland Waterways Association*, 114 Regent's Park Road, London NW1 8UQ, has leaflets and magazines about the current situation on inland waterways including restoration works and holidays. They also have a list of publications on sale.

If you are able to do so, visit the *Waterways Museum*, Stoke Bruerne, near Towcester, Northants (tel. Roade 862229). This has a unique collection of exhibits covering all aspects of canal life. It is open every day including Sundays and Bank Holidays, 10 a.m.–12.30 p.m., 2 p.m.–5 p.m., 6 p.m.–8 p.m., except for Christmas Day, Boxing Day, and on Mondays from the second Monday in October to the Monday before Good Friday, inclusive. During the period of Monday closures (that is, through the winter months) the Museum closes at 5 p.m. every day. Admission is 10p for adults and 2½p for children. You may find that you will need to visit it more than once.

Brochures about holiday boats on rivers and canals in Britain or overseas may be obtained from travel agencies.
There are several boating magazines which you might find useful. Your local newsagent might advise you of these or you could see them displayed in large newsagents' shops. You will also find local information in county magazines and local newspapers. Postcards and larger reproductions of canal paintings that are in the National Gallery can be bought from The National Gallery, Trafalgar Square, London WC2N 5DN.
Postcard views of the river or pictorial maps, can be bought at most stationery or holiday gift shops in riverside towns.

If you are writing to anyone for information, remember to write a polite letter, to mention the purpose for which you require the material and if possible, to say what it is that you are particularly looking for. It is also good manners when writing for help to enclose stamps to cover the return postage.